To bug lovers everywhere,
especially Fionn, Cillian and Nat.

BLOOMSBURY CHILDREN'S BOOKS
Bloomsbury Publishing Plc
50 Bedford Square, London, WC1B 3DP, UK

BLOOMSBURY, BLOOMSBURY CHILDREN'S BOOKS and the Diana logo are trademarks of Bloomsbury Publishing Plc

First published in Great Britain 2020 by Bloomsbury Publishing Plc

Text and illustrations copyright © Matt Robertson, 2020

Matt Robertson has asserted his right under the Copyright, Designs and Patents Act, 1988, to be identified as Author and Illustrator of this work

A catalogue record for this book is available from the British Library

ISBN: HB: 978-1-5266-0950-2; PB: 978-1-5266-0951-9; eBook: 978-1-5266-1864-1

2 4 6 8 10 9 7 5 3 1 (hardback), 2 4 6 8 10 9 7 5 3 1 (paperback)

Printed and bound in China by Leo Paper Products, Heshan, Guangdong

To find out more about our authors and books visit www.bloomsbury.com and sign up for our newsletters

DO YOU LOVE BUGS?

Matt Robertson

BLOOMSBURY
CHILDREN'S BOOKS
LONDON OXFORD NEW YORK NEW DELHI SYDNEY

Do you love bugs?

Help!

EWW!

SOME HAVE TWO EYES. SOME HAVE FIVE.

Some are **fuzzy** and **hairy**, others are simply **slimy**. Bugs can fly, crawl, wriggle and even **SOMERSAULT**! Many people are **afraid** of bugs. They flee when they see an ant ... **ARRRRGH**! They feel sick when they see a stick insect ... **EWW**!

But bugs should be **LOVED**, because they are **REALLY** important. Without bees, we wouldn't have lots of plants. Spiders do good deeds to help farmers grow their fruit and vegetables. And ants ... well, those tough little bugs have been around since the **DINOSAURS**! That makes ants **AWESOME**.

WOW!

To love a bug, remember these golden rules. Bugs are everywhere after all.

- Be careful not to bother bees.
- Show respect for the stick insect.
- No need to squirm when you see a worm.
- Give spiders a smile not a scream.
- Always be good to grasshoppers.
- Take care to step over a snail.
- Try not to bat butterflies and never make fun of moths.
- No need to dodge dragonflies.
- Never get angry at ants ...

... and BEWARE of bashing beetles.

Bees

WHY IS THAT BEE BUZZING ABOUT?

Because it's busy looking for sweet nectar, of course. YUMMY! Bees don't just make honey, they are very important for our planet. As they move from one flower to another, they collect and spread a yellow dust called pollen that helps to make new seeds. If bees didn't do this, there would be no new flowers, plants, fruit and vegetables.

So be careful not to bother bees!

When winter comes, some bees hide in old mouse holes to keep warm. Brrr!

SUPER VISION

Bumblebees and honey bees have **five** eyes. They have two big ones and three small ones.

BEE BOOGIE

Honey bees communicate with each other by dancing.

HONEY BEE

Honey bees have long, **thin** bodies and live in a hive. They are the only bees that can make honey!

BUMBLEBEE

Bumblebees have **thick**, round bodies and live in the ground. Most have black and yellow stripes, but their bottoms can be red, white, brown or yellow.

SOLD

THE LIFE OF A HONEY BEE
How honey is made

Pollen baskets

Bumblebees and honey bees store pollen in little pouches on their back legs.

Honey bees drink nectar from flowers and keep it in a separate honey stomach.

When their honey stomach is full, they return to the hive and pass the nectar to other bees. As they do this, the nectar turns to honey.

Male drone bees help the queen to make baby bees.

The queen honey bee rules the hive. She gives birth to all the baby bees.

Once the nectar turns to honey, the bees keep it safe in the hive.

Bees have two stomachs, one for storing nectar and one for eating.

Female worker bees protect the hive and look after baby bees. They also collect nectar from flowers and turn it into honey.

HONEY
One bee hive can make 80 jars of honey in a year!

Sweet!

Bees are the BEST!

Bears LOVE honey.

Stick Insects

IS IT A **LEAF?** IS IT A **TWIG?**
NO. IT'S A **STICK INSECT!**

Stick insects are the **LONGEST** bugs on our planet, but they can be the hardest to spot. Some look like bright green leaves, others look like thin brown twigs. And they rest all day, which means you will rarely see one move.

So show respect for the stick insect!

The world's longest stick insect is 62 centimetres long — that's probably about twice the length of your arm!

If I feel scared I let off a rotten smell — poooeey!

Stinky

Can you spot the stick insect?

Not me!

Try again!

Nope!

you got me!

Pick your favourite stick insect.

Watch a stick insect rock side to side like it's dancing. Lalalala!

Stick insects have been flown to new countries in planes.

NOM. NOM. NOM
Stick insects **love** plants. Their favourite leaves to munch on are **bramble**, **oak** and **hazel** leaves.

MASTER OF DISGUISE
Stick insects make a tasty snack for birds, so they must blend in with their surroundings to **protect** themselves. Some can even change colour!

I love you!

Someone's bitten my leg off!

OUCH!
If a bird attacks, stick insects **RUUUUN**! Oh dear, this one lost its leg while escaping! Don't worry, the legs of young stick insects quickly grow back.

Stick insects are SUPER!

Worms

WORMS CAN JIGGLE, TWIST, SLIIIITHER AND SOMERSAULT!

Wiggly earthworms love **digging** and **chomping** through the ground, which keeps the soil healthy, helping things to grow. Worms are also male and female at the same time and although they may seem slimy, they're actually covered in tiny hairs that help them move through the soil. They are **SUPER-BUGS**!

So no need to squirm when you SEE A WORM!

Worms can have up to FIVE hearts.

YUMMY!

Birds tap on the ground to mimic rain and trick worms into coming out so they can **EAT** them up!

Hello!

Wiggle wiggle.

7 metres

5.5 metres

BIG AND TALL

One of the biggest earthworms is the **African Giant**. It has been known to grow up to **seven metres**, which is taller than a **giraffe**!

1.15 metres

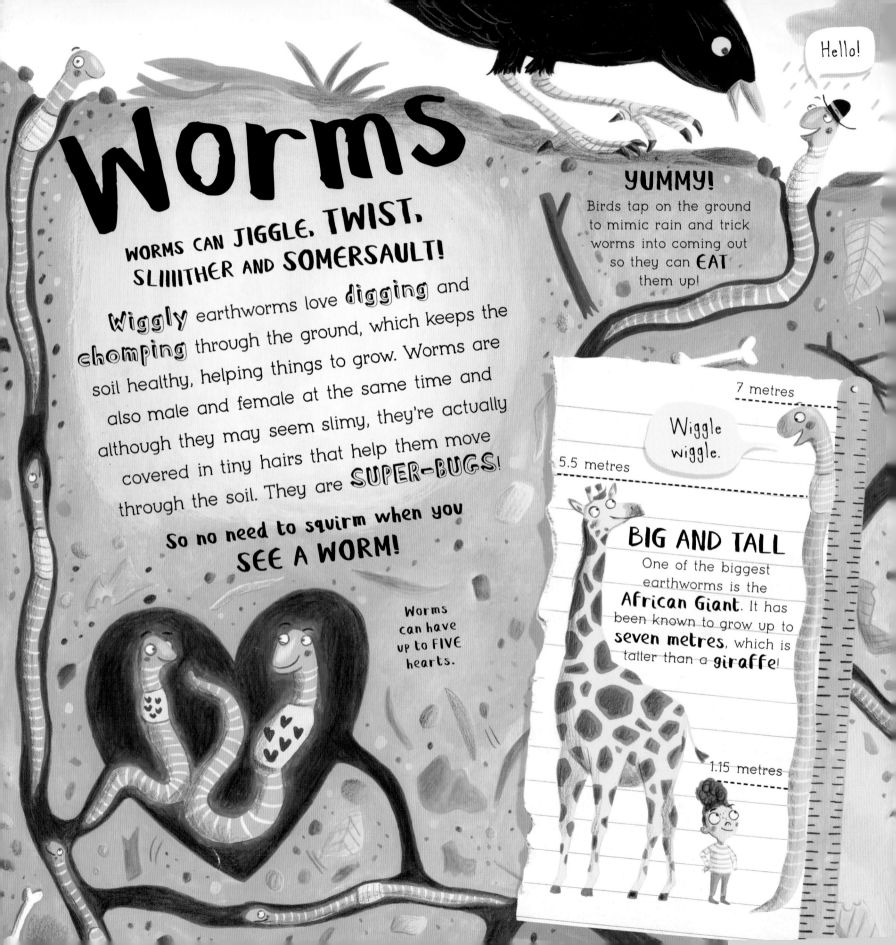

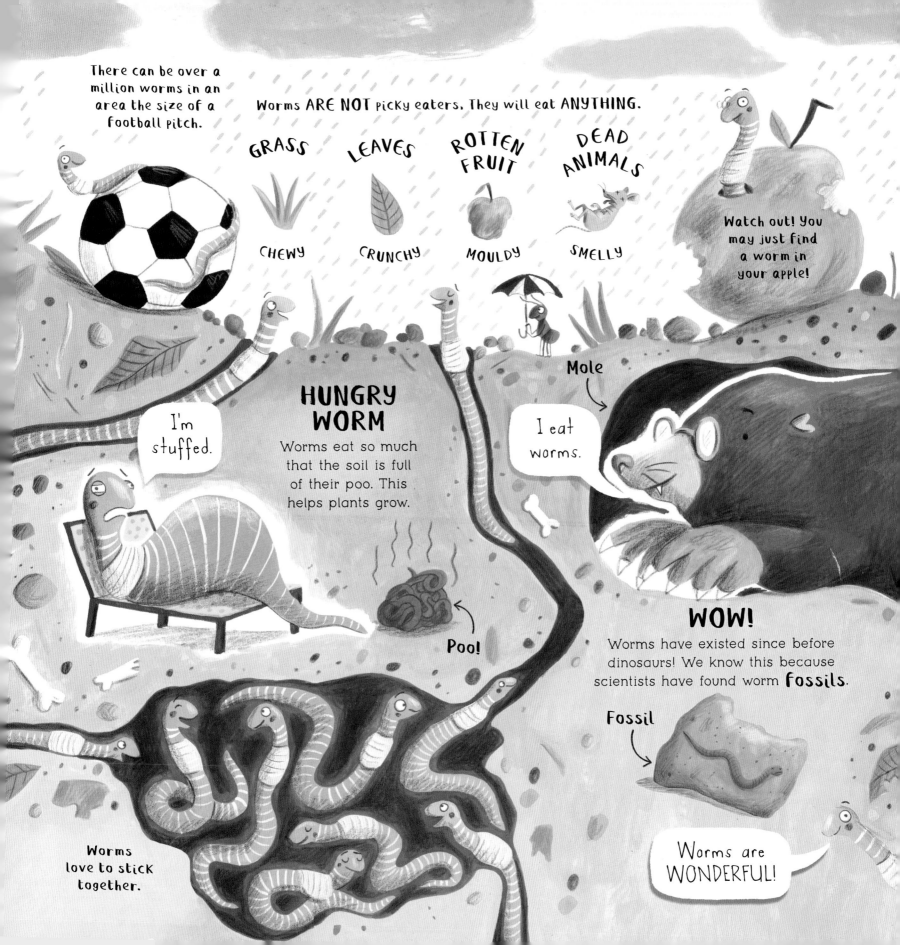

Spiders

SPIDERS ARE THE MOST AMAZING BUGS IN THE WHOLE WIDE WEB!

These **eight-legged** friends come in so many shapes and sizes. Some are BIG and **FURRY** and others are tiny and crawl about in a hurry. They can live **anywhere**, so you might not be too far from one now. Don't be scared! They may have beady eyes and sharp fangs, but they can also do cool things, like jump up high and even dance.

So give spiders a SMILE not a scream!

VEGGIE
The **Bagheera Kiplingi** spider is vegetarian. It looooves flower nectar.

I'm stuck!

Sweet!

Many spiders can hang on their silk — it looks like they are gliding through the air.

Most spiders have **EIGHT** eyes. Imagine what their glasses would look like!

C L S
K L S
Y T A B
A F W D
H M A T T P
Q R Y P A G
B G N X O L U
Z U F S A P D K L Q

Some spiders can shoot webs out of their bodies.

EYE SEE YOU!

Arachnophobic means you are REALLY scared of spiders.

SPINNING SPIDERS

Spiders **SPIN, SPIN, SPIN** silky webs to catch their dinners. The strength of their webs has been compared to **steel**. That is the material used to make big bridges.

The largest spider in the world is the Goliath birdeater. With a body size of 12 centimetres, it is bigger than both of your hands.

LOVE

Some male spiders give female spiders **gifts** to woo them. A favourite gift is flies!

I'm bubbly!

The diving bell spider lives in a bubble underwater.

SLURP!

When spiders catch their **lunch**, they turn it to mush and slurp it up. **YUK!**

Spiders eat lots of insects that are harmful to plants. Thank you, spiders!

Spiders eat more insects than birds and bats.

Spiders are SPECTACULAR!

Grasshoppers

WHAT BUG CAN JUMP HIGH AND SING AT THE SAME TIME?

Grasshoppers love to **leap** around and sing on sunny days in grassy places. So **WATCH OUT** when you go for a walk. One may spring before your eyes! Grasshoppers can be **pink**, **yellow**, **blue** ... and even **RAINBOW-coloured!** They don't bite, but when they get angry, they might **SPIT** on you!

SO always BE GOOD to grasshoppers!

Spit

Get off my grass!

BIG AND SMALL

Adult grasshoppers can grow as long as 11 centimetres, although the average is around 7 centimetres.

Grasshopper

DINOS

Grasshoppers existed long before **dinosaurs**, when huge lizards called **Pederpes** lived on Earth.

Lizard (Pederpes)

Grown-up →

Baby ←

Grasshoppers:
- See through large eyes high up on their head
- Hear through their abdomen
- Smell through their antennae
- Breathe through the side of their body

Male grasshoppers 'sing' by rubbing their back legs against their wings.

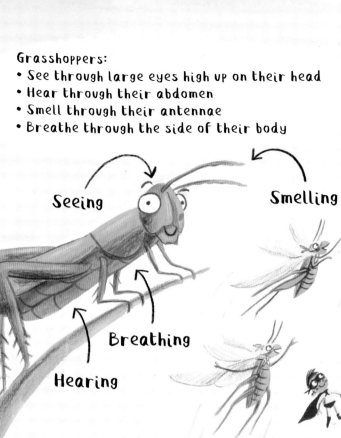

Seeing

Smelling

Breathing

Hearing

Lalala

Can you spot the rainbow-coloured grasshopper?

POO

Don't ask a grasshopper to **dinner**. It might poo as it eats!

SUPER LEAP

If you could jump like a grasshopper, you would be able to **reach** the top of a five-storey building in just one leap.

Grasshoppers are GREAT!

Snails

Boo!

SNAILS ARE SLIMY, SLOW AND STICKY.

Snails and slugs are often seen as pests to gardeners and farmers because they spend most of their time secretly munching on plants, but what other things can these amazing molluscs do? Did you know they have eyes on the ends of tentacles that they can pull back inside their head? Or that they can repair small injuries to their shell?

So take care to STEP OVER SNAILS!

Upside down

Snails create a sticky mucus called slime. This helps them to stick to anything ... and travel upside down!

The world looks funny from here!

CHOMP!

These bugs have thousands of tiny **teeth** on their tongue to help grind up their food into small pieces. Munch, munch, **MUNCH**.

Are we there yet?

It would take a snail around half an hour to travel across this page!

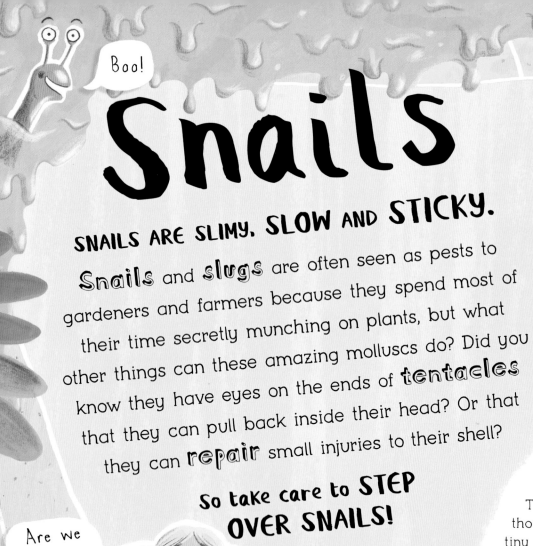

FINISH

FAMILY MATTERS

Snails belong to the family of **molluscs**, which are creatures that don't have bones! Lots of sea creatures are molluscs, like oysters, clams and shellfish.

START

BIG SNAILS
The largest snail in the world is the **Giant African Land Snail**. They grow so big that they could sit on your head like a crown.

LAZY!

I can sleep all winter in my shell.

Snails are deaf, so they wouldn't hear you even if you shouted at them.

Oi, SNAIL!

Sharing is caring.

STOP!

Snails and slugs love eating together. Some can eat up to five hundred different plants, like:

Strawberries
MUNCH!

Sunflowers
YUM!

Nettles
TASTY!

HOME SWEET HOME
A snail's shell is its home. Could you imagine carrying your **home** on your back everywhere you go?

Snails are SPECIAL!

Butterflies

PINK, BLUE, ORANGE, RED!

Butterflies are so colourful. The colour of their wings protects them from hungry animals and helps them to make new butterfly friends. They can also flap their wings 300 times in just one minute ... that's FAST! But be careful: butterfly wings are very delicate and shouldn't be touched.

So try not to BAT butterflies!

Some butterflies that live in the jungle smell just like cake.

Some people used to believe that butterflies were witches in disguise.

Butterflies love to drink nectar from sweet flowers.

Butterflies are BEAUTIFUL!

HOW BUTTERFLIES ARE BORN

YUM!

Butterflies taste with their feet.

When butterflies lay eggs on leaves, they grow into caterpillars. Caterpillars spend lots of time eating.

Then the caterpillar forms into a pupa. Inside the pupa, the caterpillar turns into a butterfly.

The butterfly now flies away.

Moths

WHY DO MOTHS COME OUT AT NIGHT?

Moths are sensitive to daylight and prefer the dark. They use **moonlight** and stars to navigate the night sky. So when you see one circling round a lamp, it's probably because it thinks it's the Moon – oops! Moths can be very clever, though. They can disguise themselves as other animals for protection.

So never make FUN of moths!

Goodnight!

Moths have thicker bodies than butterflies.

Moths are MARVELLOUS!

Tigers and tiger moths are the same colours.

Tiger

Tiger moth

Moth wings can be colourful too.

I'm fluffy.

Some moths and butterflies drink animal tears and body sweat.

Mmmm, salty!

Their fluffy bodies help keep moths warm.

Dragonflies

IS A DRAGONFLY A FIRE-BREATHING DRAGON THAT FLIES? NOOOOOOOO!

But it does fly. Really fast. Dragonflies are the speediest of all bugs. They also have amazing eyes that allow them to see all the way behind their heads. They can fly up, down and even SIDEWAYS. And they don't sting!

So no need to DODGE dragonflies. They're just Flying by!

Dragonflies grab food with their feet as they fly.

Come here!

Baby dragonflies breathe out of their bottoms. They also fart to move underwater.

The best place to spot a dragonfly is around a pond, lake or river.

Ants

ANTS ARE F-ANT-ASTIC!

Some scientists think there are so many **ants** in the world that they weigh more than all the humans put together. These tiny insects live **everywhere**, from jungles, forests and grasslands to your garden! Ants are very tidy and organised. This may have helped them survive on Earth since the **DINOSAURS**, even after a big meteor hit the planet. These are some tough little bugs.

So never get **angry** AT ANTS!

FLYING ANTS

Every summer, in the UK, winged ants fly away from their colonies to **build** new ones nearby.

I am the queen ant! And these are my worker ants.

I am a wood ant. I fire jets of stinging acid at animals that want to eat me.

ZOOOOM

Ants are super **FAST**. If they were as big as humans, they would be able to **run** as fast as a moving **car**.

Beetles

ONE IN EVERY FOUR ANIMALS ON EARTH IS A BEETLE!

There are too many to fit on one page, but here are some fun ones. Look out for colourful beetles, poo-loving beetles, big beetles and tiny beetles! They all look different but have one thing in common: their strong wings work like a shield protecting their soft and delicate body underneath.

So BEWARE of bashing beetles!

Despite their names, glow-worms are beetles. The females light up their bums to attract a mate.

Glow-worms

Jewel beetle

Red flat bark beetle

Jewel beetles can live in hot countries and red flat bark beetles can survive in very cold countries.

I wear tough armour.

Most beetles can fly!

Scydosella

The smallest beetle in the world is the Scydosella.

Titan beetle

One of the largest beetles in the world is the titan beetle.

Dung beetles

Dung beetles roll animal poo into big balls and then **eat** them.

Devil's coach horse

Devil's coach horse beetles are **stinky**.

I'm a striped beetle!

Striped cucumber beetle

Stag beetle

Stag beetles are a protected species. Take good care of any you find.

Christmas beetle

Christmas beetles only come out of the soil in Australia and South Africa around Christmas time.

Soldier beetle

Soldier beetles **love** to sit on flowers.

Ladybirds

A ladybird is a spotty beetle. Not all ladybirds are **ladies**; there are male ladybirds too.

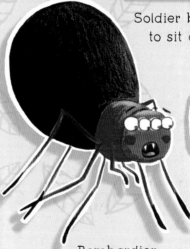

Beetles are brilliant!

Bombardier beetle

Bombardier beetles squirt **boiling hot** liquid on predators!

Bonus bugs

WAIT! DID WE FORGET SOME BUGS?

Before you close this book, say hello to these BONUS BUGS. Each one is special in its own way and plays an important role in our world.

And if you're still not sure that you **love** bugs, remember: they keep the soil healthy and plants growing. Without these furry, fuzzy, slimy friends, we wouldn't have food and the planet would be much dirtier – don't forget, worms eat rotten fruit! So let's protect our bugs and their homes. You can do this by planting new flowers, watering plants and being careful not to hurt any of these **not-so-creepy** crawlies.

Leafhoppers have special legs that allow them to jump in all directions.

Tiny water bears can survive in extreme heat AND freezing cold.

Praying mantises can turn their heads all the way round.

Hello!

Millipedes have up to 200 little legs!